Advice from a Tree ®

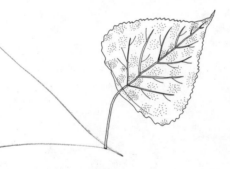

20 00
Better World Press, Inc.
Fort Collins, Colorado

Published by Better World Press, Inc.
A Division of Your True Nature, Inc.
P.O. Box 272309, Fort Collins, Colorado 80527
800-992-4769 email: grow@yourtruenature.com
Website www.yourtruenature.com

© 2000 Ilan Shamir   Advice from a Tree® is a
Registered Trademark of Your True Nature, Inc.

No part of this book may be reproduced or transmitted in any form or
by any means, electronic or mechanical, including photocopying,
recording, or by any information storage and retrieval system without
the permission in writing from the copyright holders.

Original Illustrations by Ilan Shamir
Library of Congress Cataloging-in-Publication Data
ISBN 1-930175-01-9
   Shamir, Ilan, 1951-
         Advice from a Tree / Ilan Shamir
            1. Trees   2. Human Growth and Potential
            3. Nature   4. Health & Wellness

Printed in USA on Recycled Paper. Many thanks to
the trees for their gift of paper! All paper used in the
printing of this book has been replanted through the
100% Replanted program. Visit www.ReplantTrees.org.

*E*veryone needs a wise friend. Someone who knows how to say just the right thing. At just the right moment. Here a hundred year old Cottonwood tree shares its simple wisdom about life, about living in harmony with ourselves and with nature.

I walked by this giant Cottonwood tree many times. Many times I've appreciated its shade on a hot summer's day, enjoyed the leaves twirling in the wind as they return to earth in October, and pondered what stories this tree could tell from just one of its more than forty thousand days and nights watching over this neighborhood.

Today was different. I stopped. As I leaned against the tree the words seemed to flow out of me as I said, *"Can you help me? I need some advice!"* I felt the tree reach out to me, to wrap me in its branches, invite me closer and comfort me as I leaned against its steady trunk. This old and wise Cottonwood tree spoke to me with kindness and wisdom.

Advice from a Tree...

Stand Tall
and Proud!

Sink your Roots Deeply into the Earth

Reflect the Light
of Your Own
True Nature!

Once a very old man
was planting trees.
Someone came up to him and said,
"Why are you planting trees?
You will never be around
to see them mature."
His reply was simple,
"I do not plant them for myself,
I plant them for future generations!"
... As a child he had so much
enjoyed the magnificence
of the trees that had been planted
years before that he wanted
to show his appreciation
and give the earth
his own special gift.

Think
Long
Term

Go Out on a Limb

Remember
Your Place
Among
All
Living Beings

Embrace with Joy the Changing Seasons

For Each
Yields its own
Abundance

The Energy and Birth of Spring!

The Growth and Contentment of Summer

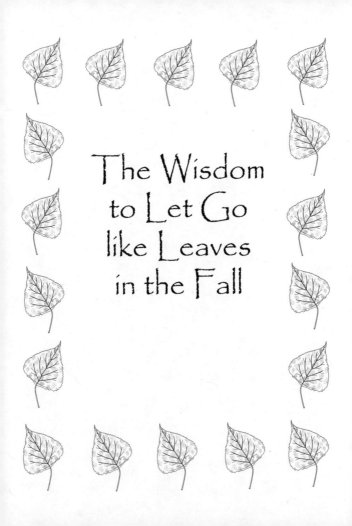

The Rest and Quiet Renewal of Winter

Feel the Wind
and the Sun
and Delight
in Their Presence

Look up at the
Moon that Shines
Down Upon You

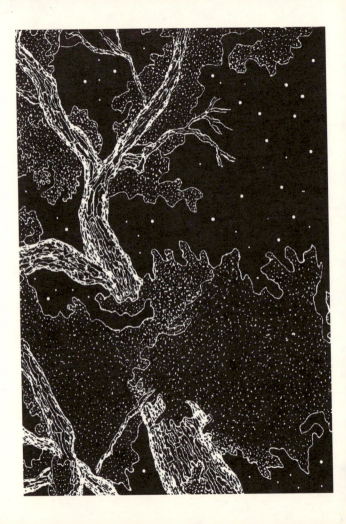

And the Mystery
of the Stars
at Night

Seek Nourishment from Good Things in Life

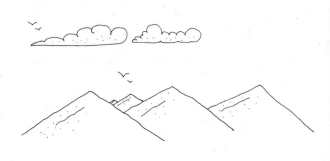

Simple Pleasures

Earth
Fresh Air
Light

Be Content
with Your
Natural
Beauty

Drink Plenty of Water

Let Your Limbs Sway and Dance in the Breezes

Be Flexible

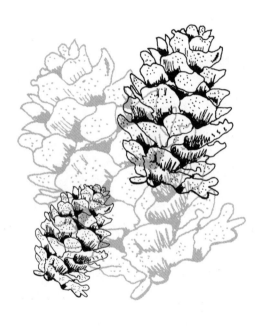

Remember
Your
Roots

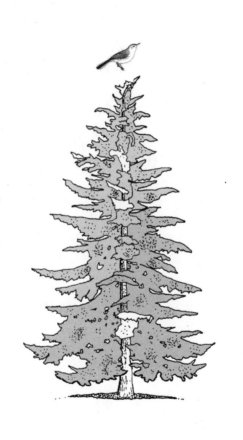

Enjoy
the
View!

Advice From a Tree

Dear Friend,
Stand Tall and Proud

Sink your Roots
deeply into the Earth

Reflect the Light
of your own
True Nature

Think long term

Go out on a Limb

Remember your place
among All living beings

Embrace with Joy
the changing seasons

For each yields its own abundance

The Energy and Birth of Spring

The Growth and Contentment of Summer

The Wisdom to let go like leaves in the Fall

The Rest and Quiet Renewal of Winter

Feel the wind and the sun
And delight in their presence

Look up at the moon that shines down upon you
And the mystery of the stars at night

Seek Nourishment from the Good Things in life
Simple pleasures
Earth,
Fresh Air, Light

Be Content
with your natural beauty

Drink plenty of Water

Let your limbs sway
and dance in the breezes

Be flexible

Remember your Roots!

Enjoy the View!

Ilan Shamir

About the Author

Ilan Shamir lives in Colorado, among the fluttering Aspen trees and uplifting Rocky Mountains. His love of trees came early in life, when his Aunt and Uncle gave him the precious gift of a Magnolia tree for his birthday as a young child. To replant the many trees used in his successful book publishing and greeting card company, Ilan created Fort Collins Re-Leaf in 1990 with Gregory Long. The organization has planted and celebrated more than thirty thousand trees in Colorado, including "TreeHenge" in Fort Collins, a living re-creation of Stonehenge in England.

Ilan's journeys have taken him to ancient and historic trees all over the world, leading wilderness expeditions in the Swiss Alps and a 40 day solo across remote Iceland.

He has studied with Don Jose Matsuwa, a one-hundred-year-old elder, in the Mexican village of the Huichol Indians and has learned the craft of making Cottonwood tree drums with Red Shirt at the Taos Pueblo.

Ilan brings to life the wisdom and beauty of nature and the teachings of the wise elders through "Advice from a Tree" storytelling/drumming performances, keynotes and workshops.

"There are many role models in life to choose from ... for me I look up to the trees! By standing proud and simple upon the earth, trees guide me to live in harmony with myself and with all of life."

Ilan Shamir

Ilan Shamir

Programs and Products for Conferences and Events!

* *Keynote Programs*
* *Workshops*
* *Storytelling Performances*
* *Tree Planting & Celebrations*

Through the simplicity and beauty of trees and nature, Ilan Shamir calls us to branch out, grow and celebrate our true nature! Author of the bestselling *Advice from a Tree*® products and *A Thousand Things Went Right Today*®, Ilan's inspiring programs and products will delight all ages!

Member:
*National Associaton for Interpretation
*National Speakers Association
*National Storytellers Network

www.YourTrueNature.com

Have a Tree Planted for Someone Special!

Your purchase price of $8.95 for one tree, or $18.95 for a three tree grove, plants and cares for this living gift in a protected watershed area by the non-profit organization Trees, Water and People. Currently native trees are being planted in El Salvador including Mahogany, Leucaena, Pine and Cedar and will be planted for any occasion you choose. Here's the great part. The recipient not only gets a beautiful personalized greeting card from you, but both you and the recipient can visit the planting area online!

A simple gift that lasts a lifetime!

It's as easy as 1, 2, TREE ...

QTY ($8.95)	QTY ($18.95)	OCCASION
___	___	Birthday
___	___	Friendship
___	___	Memorial
___	___	Holiday
___	___	All Occasion
___	___	Birth
___	___	Anniversary
___	___	Wedding
___	___	Graduation
___	___	Congratulations
___	___	Fathers Day
___	___	Mothers Day
___	___	Thank You

Your Name _____
Address _____
City/State/Zip _____
Email _____
Telephone _____

Total Qty ____ at $ 8.95 = $_____
Total Qty ____ at $18.95 = $_____
      Shipping $ 6.50
      GRAND TOTAL $_____

Send with your check to:
Your True Nature, Inc. Box 272309,
Ft Collins, CO 80527, (970)282-1620,
Email us at grow@yourtruenature.com.
Visit our website for more information or to order online at http://www.yourtruenature.com

When you plant a tree,
you'll grow a friend,
a friend you'll have
for life!

Ilan Shamir